BRANDENBURGER

IMAGES OF WAR

BRANDENBURGER

WARTIME PHOTOGRAPHS OF WILHELM WALTHER

Anthony Rogers

Greenhill Books

First published in Great Britain in 2022 by

Greenhill Books

c/o Pen & Sword Books Ltd, 47 Church Street, Barnsley,
South Yorkshire, S70 2AS, England
For more information on our books, please visit
www.greenhillbooks.com, email contact@greenhillbooks.com
or write to us at the above address.

ISBN 978-1-78438-715-0

A CIP catalogue record for this book is available from the British Library.

Typeset in Gill Sans by Concept, Huddersfield, West Yorkshire, HD4 5JL
Printed and bound by CPI Group (UK) Ltd, Croydon, CR0 4YY

FSC
www.fsc.org
MIX
Paper from responsible sources
FSC® C013604

Contents

Introduction

This book in no way purports to be a history of what would evolve as the Division 'Brandenburg'. It is, quite simply, a pictorial record of the campaigns and operations of one 'Brandenburger', Wilhelm 'Uwe' Walther, represented by a selection of some of the 600 images from his personal photo album. It is presented as a tribute to the life and times of a career officer, whose military service, like so many of his generation, ended abruptly at the end of the Second World War.

This project can be said to have originated when I interviewed Uwe during the course of researching my book *Churchill's Folly*. This covers events in the Aegean in the autumn of 1943, in which units of the Division 'Brandenburg' participated. At his home in Heidelberg, I was provided with a glimpse of Uwe's photo album and saw then the potential for a unique book. Uwe died on 25 November 2010, age 100. Many years later, the photo album was rediscovered in the safekeeping of one of his sons, Andreas. Eventually, after much negotiating, I was able to borrow the album and scan the images therein. The successful negotiation was achieved largely as a result of the tact and diplomacy of my good friend in Bavaria, Hans Peter Eisenbach.

Photographs span the pre-war years through to August 1944. If later images exist, it is not known what became of them. A collection of wartime colour slides, together with documentation, is no longer accessible, having been acquired by a collector.

Original captions, written on album pages or the backs of photographs, were transcribed by my dear friend Bettina Selke in Berlin. This involved painstakingly deciphering old-style *Sütterlinschrift*. Bettina also undertook her own independent research to provide much additional information.

Photographs in the album are displayed somewhat haphazardly. In nearly all cases, captions are brief, place names are often not included and there are few dates. I have attempted to redress this, wherever possible, by rearranging images chronologically, by particular campaigns, or regionally. For authenticity, I have included the original captions, exactly as they were written, together with English translations, ably assisted in this regard by Kuno Gross in Switzerland.

Jason Mark in Australia assisted in identifying individuals in a number of images, and Hugo van Dijk in Holland provided invaluable documents, including Wilhelm Walther's after-action report of the 10 May 1940 Gennep operation.

My thanks and appreciation to all who helped bring this project to fruition, and especially to Marita and Andreas Walther for kindly granting access to the photo album and for their hospitality during my visit to their hometown in Germany.

Generalleutnant a.D.Traut

61 Darmstadt, den 27.3.66
Heinrichstr. 7

Herrn
Oberstleutnant a.D. Wilhelm W a l t h e r
6906 L e i m e n üb. Heidelberg
Lingentaler Hof

Sehr geehrter Herr Walther!

Vor einiger Zeit hat mir Herr Direktor a.D. H.Seifert, Darmstadt, Kröh= weg 3,das anliegende Foto-Album mit der Bitte übergegen, ob ich nicht Name u. Anschrift des Besitzers - falls er gefallen, vermißt oder ver= storben sein sollte, seiner Angehörigen - ausfindig machen könnte. Sein Sohn Hanno habe das Album 1945 in einer Truhe eines leerstehenden Gebäudes an der Nibelungenstr. in oder bei Bensheim a.D.Bergstr. ent= deckt u. an sich genommen, damit es die Amerikaner bei ihrem bevor= stehenden Eintreffen nicht fänden.
Es ist der Wunsch von Herrn Seifert u. Sohn, daß das Album mit seinen für den Eigentümer bzw. seine Angehörige wertvollen Aufnahmen wieder in die richtigen Hände kommt.

Zu meiner Entlastung u. um Familie Seifert benachrichtigen zu können, darf ich wohl um Bestätigung des Empfanges bitten.

Sollten Sie wider Erwarten nicht der Eigentümer sein u. ihn auch nicht kennen, bitte ich um Rücksendung. Sollten Sie den Eigentümer kennen, wäre ich für Weiterleitung dankbar.

Mit kameradschaftlichen Grüßen

Ihr

Traut

(**Opposite**) *This letter, dated 27 March 1966, is affixed to a page at the start of Wilhelm Walther's photo album. Ritterkreuzträger (Knight's Cross holder) Generalleutnant Hans Traut was an infantry division commander when taken prisoner by the Soviets in July 1944. He remained in captivity until 1955.*

Dear Mr Walther!

Some time ago, former Director H. Seifert, Darmstadt, Kröhweg 3, gave me the attached photo album with the request whether I could find the name and address of the owner, and, if he was killed in action, missing or deceased, of his relatives.
His son Hanno had discovered the album in 1945 in a chest of an empty building in Niebelungenstrasse in or near Bensheim an der Bergstrasse and had taken it so that the Americans would not find it when they arrived.
It is the wish of Mr Seifert and his son that the album, with its valuable recordings for the owner or his relatives, will be returned to the right hands.

For my own relief and in order to be able to inform the Seifert family, I would like to ask for confirmation of receipt.

If, contrary to expectations, you are not the owner and do not know him, please return it to me. If you know the owner, I would be grateful if you could forward it to him.

With comradely greetings

Yours

[*signed* Traut]

Wilhelm Walther.

Wilhelm Walther and the 'Brandenburger'

In comparison with other units of the Second World War, relatively little has been written about Germany's wartime commandos, better known as the Brandenburger, and what there is varies in quality and reliability. This is hardly surprising, considering the paucity of source material available to researchers and the air of mystery and intrigue still surrounding this unique formation.

What would eventually become a *Panzergrenadier* division owes its origins to the pre-war Abwehr – German Military Intelligence – and the creation of an initially small force for clandestine missions in enemy territory. This, the brainchild of Hauptmann (Captain) Dr. Theodor von Hippel, was ably supported by Major Helmuth Groscurth, his former head at Abteilung II, the department responsible for sabotage and insurrection. Abwehr chief, Admiral Wilhelm Canaris, less than keen to begin with, was soon won over, allowing the concept to be developed and taken forward. He would have his own agenda, however.

If Hippel did not think highly of National Socialism, both Canaris and Groscurth were actively opposed to Adolf Hitler. Canaris, in particular, seems to have viewed a commando unit as a useful tool in the unlikely event of a putsch leading to the downfall of Germany's Führer. Of the three, just one would survive the war. In 1943, Hippel, by this time an *Oberstleutnant* (lieutenant colonel), was taken prisoner by the Americans in North Africa. By the beginning of 1939, Groscurth had been reassigned. He was an *Oberst* (colonel) assigned to XI. Armeekorps as Chief of Staff when he surrendered to Russian forces at Stalingrad in 1943. He died from typhus a few weeks later. Admiral Canaris would be implicated in the 20 July 1944 bomb plot to kill Hitler and, after being imprisoned and tortured, was one of seven conspirators executed at Flossenbürg concentration camp in the last weeks of the war.

Initially, Abwehr commandos were linked with another clandestine organisation – Ebbinghaus. The first tasks were undertaken during the occupation of Poland in 1939, with personnel, posing as civilians, securing key points preparatory to the arrival of regular forces. After the Polish campaign, the Abwehr element was retained, undergoing a number of changes before emerging, in January 1940, as Bau-Lehr-Bataillon z.b.V. 800. This was a deliberately misleading title: *Bau Lehr* can be translated as 'construction teaching' and z.b.V. – *zur besonderen Verwendung* – 'for special use'. The number 800 was allocated simply because it was available. Based at Brandenburg an der Havel, west of Berlin, the unit soon adopted the name of the garrison, and was redesignated Lehr-Regiment 'Brandenburg' z.b.V. 800, in June 1940.

Among early recruits was a 30-year-old army officer from Dresden. Wilhelm Walther was so christened after being born on 27 January 1910 – the same birthday as the German emperor, Wilhelm II. The son of an innkeeper, 'Uwe', as he would later be known, enjoyed a middle-class family upbringing. After attaining his *Abitur* (high school certificate) in 1929, he attended university, where he studied architecture and became active in the Burschenschaft Cheruscia (a student fraternity). He also joined the paramilitary Grenzschutz (border protection), heading an unofficial student company. Young Walther evidently possessed martial qualities that did not go unnoticed. In November 1933, on the recommendation of the *Sturmabteilung-Hochschulamt* (Storm Division/SA-High School Department), he was appointed military sports instructor at the University of Hamburg, and, between mid-January 1933 and the end of October 1934, headed the *SA-Sportschule* (SA Sport School) at nearby Trittau, where he was awarded the SA-Sportabzeichen in Gold (SA Sports Badge in Gold). At age 24, he joined the Reichswehr (shortly to be reorganised as the Wehrmacht).

Walther was a reserve *Feldwebel* (sergeant), prior to being commissioned on 1 June 1936 as a reserve *Leutnant* (second lieutenant) in Aufklärungs-Abteilung 5 (A.A.5), an armoured reconnaissance unit in 2. Panzer-Division. He became a regular *Leutnant* in June 1937, being promoted to *Oberleutnant* (first lieutenant) on 1 October 1938. At the outbreak of the Second World War, he was a *Kompanie Führer*, taking part in the Polish campaign. His primary employment as a staff officer, however, was not to his liking. Keen to see more action, Walther applied for a transfer to the *Fallschirmjäger* (paratroopers). Prevented from leaving by his commanding officer, he asked if he might instead join the Luftwaffe (air force) to train as a *Schlachtflieger* (ground-attack pilot). This, too, was refused. So, Walther telephoned a friend, former-A.A.5 officer Dietrich Witzel, then serving in another, little-known, unit. Witzel urged Walther to put his name forward, only saying that his new employer would be the Abwehr. Without any real idea of what he was letting himself in for, Walther did so and, this time, he was successful. Canaris himself had approved the request, overruling any further objections by Walther's CO.

Wilhelm Walther was assigned to 4. Kompanie, Bau-Lehr-Bataillon z.b.V. 800 on 15 March 1940. He was *Kompanie Führer* until 31 May, by which time he had become the first of his unit to receive the coveted Ritterkreuz (Knight's Cross).

The first task for Oberleutnant Walther after joining the battalion was to secure one of a series of objectives in the Netherlands preparatory to the German invasion of that country. On 10 May 1940, he led a small team in seizing a railway bridge, some 300 metres in length, that spanned the River Meuse near the town of Gennep.

The initial strength of the commando group was probably no more than a dozen in total. This included three Dutch *Kampfdolmetscher* (combat interpreters) wearing German-manufactured *Koninklijke Marechaussee* (gendarmerie) uniforms. Walther and his German contingent were their 'prisoners' – with sub-machine guns concealed beneath long coats, six stick grenades slung behind their backs, and with egg grenades in each man's gas mask canister and *Brotbeutel* ('bread bag'). In the early hours of the morning, the team was taken by lorry towards the German–Dutch border.

There, one of the Dutch volunteers asked to withdraw. He was disarmed and held at a German border post. The remainder continued on foot. After some two and a half hours, when just short of their objective, Walther called a halt and observed what lay ahead: a defence system that included concrete bunkers and a numerically superior local guard force. After half an hour, Walther and his team broke cover, advancing in plain view. Exactly what occurred next is debatable. On reaching the bridge, there was some sort of scuffle and several guards were overpowered. This enabled a *Feldwebel* to enter the guardhouse, where he set to severing telephone wires. While this was taking place, someone at the far end of the bridge opened fire, wounding another *Feldwebel* in the hand. Leaving two team members with their Dutch prisoners and the lightly wounded man, Walther and the others pressed on. Midway, more wires were seen and surreptitiously cut. For whatever reason, the small group met with no further opposition until they neared the opposite side, when they encountered a guard force of platoon-strength, if not more. The Dutchmen seemed hesitant, clearly uncertain how to deal with such a situation. After only a cursory search, five men took charge of the 'prisoners', leading them towards the western bridgehead. At the same time, one of Walther's Dutchmen returned the way he had come, with the pretext of collecting his bicycle, and joined the team members there.

Walther's mission was not going well. He and his men – only four or five at this stage – were covered by their escorts' rifles and so prevented from producing their own weapons. Just when it seemed that the mission had failed, Walther noticed in the distance what he took to be steam from an expected German armoured train. Seizing the initiative, he shouted a warning: '*Panzerzug von hinten, volle Deckung!*' ('Armoured train behind, get under cover!'). This had the desired effect, distracting the guards and enabling the Germans to escape and take up firing positions. Meanwhile, those at the eastern bridgehead began to shift a heavy barrier, to clear the way for the approaching armoured train. This was achieved under fire, during which an *Obergefreiter* was badly wounded.

The train arrived with German troops, some of whom joined in the shooting, misidentifying Walther and his men. Walther was wounded and left momentarily partially deaf when a round pierced the right side of his helmet. After the mistake was realised and the situation brought under control, remaining bunkers were cleared, sometimes while under German artillery fire, and by about 06:00 it was all over. An estimated thirty to forty Dutch prisoners had been taken, apparently without fatalities on either side.

For his performance, on 24 May Oberleutnant Walther was decorated with the Ritterkreuz. Years later, he explained: 'By crossing the Gennep bridge, 9. Panzer-Division was able to set off for the *Peelstellung* [defence line] and, after a successful breakthrough, was able to establish contact with the *Fallschirmjäger* who had landed near Moerdjik as early as 12 May. Thus, the southern entrance way to "Fortress Holland" was firmly in German hands.' The operation would be used as an example during future training for 'Brandenburg' troops, demonstrating, as it did, the ability to think fast and improvise and never to accept defeat, whatever the odds.

On 1 June 1940, Walther became a *Kompanie-Chef* in II. Bataillon of what was now Lehr-Regiment 'Brandenburg' z.b.V. 800, being appointed I. Bataillon *Führer* on 16 September. He was promoted to *Hauptmann* on 1 March 1941. In April, he took part in Operation 'Marita' and the Balkans Campaign – the occupation of Greece and Yugoslavia. Operation 'Barbarossa' – the German invasion of Russia – followed in June.

Walther was employed as liaison officer with Panzergruppe 4, probably until mid-August, when he is believed to have returned to Germany and been hospitalised at Darmstadt. On 1 November, he resumed his previous role at I. Bataillon. After a spell of home duty, Walther returned to Russia, where he remained for some eight months, until 9 February 1943 – serving initially as *Kommandeur* Bataillon I. (1 April 1942 to 19 November 1942). Subordinated to Heeresgruppe B (Army Group B), Walther's battalion was at the forefront of the push towards Stalingrad, and for some time operated as an ad-hoc battle formation: 'Gruppe Walther'.

By this time, the *Sicherheitsdienst des Reichsführers-SS* (SD – Security Service of the Reichsführer-SS) – rightly considered by Hitler as being more dependable than many in the rival Abwehr – were also engaged in clandestine tasks not dissimilar to those undertaken by the Brandenburger. In April 1943, SS-Obersturmführer (SS First Lieutenant) Otto Skorzeny would be appointed commander of the SS special force.

Such a development clearly represented a threat to the continued existence of the Abwehr commandos. As it was, they were no longer being utilised to their full potential, but instead were being increasingly employed at precarious sectors of the front. It was decided to expand and reorganise the force, which, in January 1943, became Sonderverbandes 'Brandenburg'. Five *Verbänden* would provide the nucleus of the restructured formation (Walther having been appointed in November 1942 to command Verband 801, formerly I. Bataillon). In April 1943, the Brandenburger were subordinated to the Oberkommando der Wehrmacht (OKW – Armed Forces High Command)/Wehrmachtführungsstab (Armed Forces Command Staff), leaving only an independent Lehr-Regiment 'Kurfürst' under Abwehr control. The *Verbänden* and their parent unit were also redesignated. Verband 801 became Jägerregiment 1 'Brandenburg' of what was now the Division 'Brandenburg'. Significantly, the suffix z.b.V. no longer applied.

Walther was promoted to *Major* on 1 February 1943, and in June 1943 returned to Russia, this time to the Leningrad area. After only a few weeks, he was redeployed to Greece. There, his command was involved in the seizure of the Dodecanese from British and Italian forces, concluding with Walther negotiating the Italian surrender of the island of Samos on 22 November 1943. Following anti-guerrilla operations in mainland Greece in early 1944, Jägerregiment 1 moved to Yugoslavia. In May/June 1944, newly promoted Oberstleutnant Walther participated in Operation 'Rösselsprung' ('Knight's Move'), the main objective of which was to kill or capture Josip Broz Tito. Notwithstanding the resources and manpower involved, the undertaking failed, and Tito was airlifted to safety (subsequently re-establishing his headquarters on the Adriatic island of Vis).

An increasingly mistrustful Hitler had in the meantime reassigned the functions of the Abwehr to the Reichssicherheitshauptamt (RSHA – Reich Security Main Office). Canaris had been sacked and replaced by Oberst Georg Hansen, a fellow conspirator in the German anti-Nazi movement – also soon to be arrested in the wake of the 20 July 1944 bomb plot. What, then, was to become of the Brandenburger?

In summer 1944, the division was again reorganised to include several *Streifkorps* (raiding force units) and in August, the 'Brandenburg' cuff title was introduced. This was an honour bestowed upon the most elite formations, as well as those who had participated in notable campaigns. A number of Brandenburger, among them Oberstleutnant Walther, were invited to Berlin and hosted by the Reich Propaganda Minister Dr. Joseph Goebbels. The following month, the division was subordinated to the Oberkommando des Heeres (OKH – Army High Command)/Generalstab des Heeres (Army General Staff). The majority of Brandenburger would go on to serve as regular infantry in what became Panzergrenadier-Division 'Brandenburg', soon to join Panzergrenadier-Division 'Großdeutschland' to form Panzerkorps 'Großdeutschland'. Hundreds of disaffected Brandenburger, hoping to continue in a familiar role, and irrespective of their politics, opted to join SS-Obersturmbannführer (SS Lieutenant Colonel) Otto Skorzeny's SS-Jagdverbände, which had effectively replaced the old-style Brandenburger. Only the 'Brandenburg' *Kustenjäger* (coastal assault force) and *Fallschirmjäger* would retain their autonomous status.

For a while, Oberstleutnant Walther continued to serve in the Panzergrenadier-Division 'Brandenburg'. On 1 October 1944, he was severely wounded as the Russians closed in on Groß Betschkerek (today Zrenjanin, Serbia), where ethnic German residents would soon suffer a terrible ordeal under Tito's partisans.

With his role as regimental commander having passed to Oberst Erich von Brückner, Walther would spend several months convalescing in hospitals in Austria and Germany. He would not resume command. Deemed fit to return to active duty, in March 1945 Walther joined the SS-Jagdverbände as Skorzeny's Chief of Staff, having replaced another former Brandenburger, Adrian Freiherr von Foelkersam, lost in action in January that year.

SS-Obersturmbannführer Skorzeny had a high regard for his Chief of Staff; Walther less so for Skorzeny, commenting many years later: 'In my eyes, he was not at all an officer.' Neither did Walther rate the SS-Jagdverbände, considering them amateurs in comparison with the now-defunct 'Brandenburg' commandos.

After a brief period at the front on the Oder, north-east of Berlin, Walther undertook his final task. Together with Skorzeny, he saw out the rest of the war in Austria, as part of *Führungsgruppe* (Lead Group) of Schutzkorps Alpenland (SKA – Alpine Region Protection Corps), in the forlorn hope of organising a guerrilla action against the advancing Allied forces. Soon after, Germany surrendered.

On 8 May 1945, Walther attempted to conceal his association with Skorzeny and the Waffen-SS. He obtained a *Soldbuch* (paybook) in the name of Uwe Schütze and set out for Jugenheim, south of Frankfurt am Main, intending to rejoin his family, but a motoring accident resulted in his being hospitalised for several weeks. Discharged by American authorities at Fürstenfeldbruck in July, 'Uwe Schütze' continued north to Stuttgart. For a while, at least, his ruse had worked.

Many Brandenburger had little choice in their fate. As part of Panzerkorps 'Großdeutschland', elements of Panzergrenadier-Division 'Brandenburg' fought costly delaying actions against the Soviets. An unknown number escaped annihilation or an uncertain future as prisoners of war by withdrawing via the Baltic to British-occupied northern Germany. Those who survived Soviet captivity returned home only after several years.

In June 1946, Wilhelm Walther was arrested at Annaberg, Austria, by the United States Army Counter Intelligence Corps. Transferred to Glasenbach, near Salzburg, in August, then to Ludwigsburg, north of Stuttgart, in November, prisoner 29-15886 eventually arrived in February 1947 at Dachau.

Extremely fortunate to have avoided extradition to Yugoslavia, where the authorities wanted to try him for alleged war crimes, Walther was instead transported to the Netherlands. Eventually, it was decided that there was no case for prosecution. On 17 May 1950, Wilhelm Walther was deported back to Germany, a free man.

The old Brandenburger would always consider his arrest and incarceration as unjust. As far as he was concerned, he had done nothing wrong; he had merely fulfilled his duty as an officer and a soldier.

Chapter One

1931–39

als Führer der Studenten Kp. in Grenzschutz [Zeithain in herbst] 1931.
As leader of the Student Company in Grenzschutz [Zeithain, autumn] 1931.

(**Above**) als Wehramtsleiter der Dresdener Studentsch. z. Turnfest i. Stuttg. [Juli] 33

As head of the defence department of the Dresden student body for the Gymnastics Festival in Stuttgart [July] 1933

The duelling scar, a result of 'academic fencing', was a mark of honour among the social elite.

(**Opposite**) Oblt. z. See a. D. G. Erdmann väterl. Freund u. Kamerad Vorgesetzter im Grenzschutz und bei der AA5. Urheber u. Gründer meiner mil. Laufbahn. Gefallen als Kdr. einer Pz AA 1940 in Frankreich b. Lille.

Oberleutnant zur See a. D. G. Erdmann, fatherly friend and comrade. My supervisor during Grenzschutz [border protection] and when with the A.A.5. Inspiration for and origin of my military career. Fell [in] 1940 as commander of a Panzer A.A. near Lille in France.

On the back of this photograph there is written:

dem Studenten Wilhelm Walther in dankbarer Anerkennung seiner Leistungen in dreijähriger Zusammenarbeit von seinem alten Kameraden
Erdmann
Weihnachten 1933

The student Wilhelm Walther in grateful recognition of his achievements during three years of cooperation from his old comrade
Erdmann
Christmas 1933

A naval officer previously, Major (promoted posthumously to Oberstleutnant) Günther Erdmann was killed in France on 28 May 1940, while commanding the armoured reconnaissance unit, Panzer-Aufklärungs-Abteilung 37.

(**Above**) BESETZUNG DES SUDENLANDES [sic: SUDETENLANDES]
1. – 8. SEPTEMBER [sic] 1938
AM GRENZÜBERGANG

OCCUPATION OF THE SUDETENLAND
1–8 SEPTEMBER [sic] 1938
AT THE BORDER CROSSING

This and the next two photographs were taken on 8 October 1938, probably at Lichtenau (Lichkov in present-day Czech Republic), when Wilhelm Walther was a newly promoted Oberleutnant in Aufklärungs-Abteilung 5.

„BLUMENKRIEG"

[*Lit.*] 'FLOWERS WAR' *or* 'WAR OF FLOWERS'

(**Opposite**) Auf die Minute genau überschreitet der erste vorst. Spähtr. der Abt. die Tschech. Grenzen. 8.10.38.

On the minute, the first advancing reconnaissance patrol of the *Abteilung* crosses the Czech border. 8 October 1938.

(**Below**) Das waren die ersten deutschen Soldaten, die dieser „Bunker" sah. 8.10.38.
These were the first German soldiers to see this 'bunker' on 8 October 1938.

(**Above**) Für den Pi-Zug der A.A.5 gab es immer Abwechslung u. Arbeit. 8.10.38.
For the Pioneer Platoon of A.A.5 there was always variety and work. 8 October 1938.

(**Below**) SO SAHEN DIE AUS, DIE EINE DEUTSCHE WEHRMACHT SCHLAGEN WOLLTEN
WHAT THEY WHO WANTED TO DEFEAT A GERMAN WEHRMACHT LOOK LIKE

(**Below and the following five images**) TSCHECHISCHE GRENZFESTUNGEN
CZECH BORDER FORTIFICATIONS

Vorm Schloß des Fürsten Lichtenstein [sic: Liechtenstein]
In front of the castle of Liechtenstein princes
Valtice Castle in present-day Czech Republic.

(**Below**) *Vranov Dam in the Czech Republic, on the southern border with Austria.*

Translation: To the front.

8.10.38. Da nützt das Fäuste ballen auch nichts, erst muß sich Bert [Kuntz] mit einem tschech. Stahlhelm mal fotografieren lassen. Zum Trost darf der Tschech die Panzermütze mal aufsetzen.

8 October 1938. Clenching your fists is of no use either. First, Bert [Kuntz] has to be photographed wearing a Czech steel helmet. As consolation, the Czech is allowed to put on his tank cap.

(**Above**) And the truth has won after all!

Built by French money and Czech megalomania, this bunker was visited on 26 October 1938 by the creator of Greater Germany and saviour of the Sudeten Germans, Adolf Hitler.

(**Opposite above**) Offizier-Korps der Pz. AA5 1938 unter Obstlt. [sic: Major] Kitschmann

Officer corps of Panzer-Aufklärungs-Abteilung 5 [in] 1938 under Oberstleutnant [sic: Major] Kitschmann

Major (Oberstleutnant from September 1939) Horst Kitschmann commanded Aufklärungs-Abteilung 5 – later re-designated Panzer-Aufklärungs-Abteilung 5.

Stab

(**Above**) *Christmas, 1938.*

(**Below and the following seven pages**) BESETZUNG MÄHRENS UND BÖHMENS MÄRZ 1939

OCCUPATION OF MORAVIA AND BOHEMIA, MARCH 1939

EINZUG IN BRÜNN

ENTERING BRNO

186

LAHUDKY

KRIEGSSCHULLEHRGANG I. MÜNCHEN
WARFARE COURSE IN MUNICH

12 STUNDEN ALPENFERNFAHRT 1939

12 HOURS ALPINE TRIP 1939

The 'Internationale Deutsche Alpenfahrt 1939' (International German Alpine Tour) started from Munich, with participants on motorcycles and in cars, covering 1,600 kilometres in three days.

(**Above**) MEINE GARNISON EGGENBURG/NIEDERDONAU
AUG. 38 – 19. AUG. 39
MY GARRISON EGGENBURG/NIEDERDONAU
AUGUST 1938–19 AUGUST 1939

(**Opposite below and this page above**) NACHRICHTENÜBUNG IM SALZKAMMERGUT SOMMER 1939

NACHRICHTENÜBUNG [REPORTING EXERCISE] IN THE SALZKAMMERGUT SUMMER 1939

WH-179015

WH-179022

Chapter Two

1940

Kurz vor 10.4.40. in der Eifel

Shortly before 10 April 1940 in the Eifel

Probably in the area of Kaisersesch, south-west of Koblenz.

Die Brücke über die Maas b. Gennep nach verhinderter Sprengung am 10.5.1940 in der Hauptstoßrichtung der 18. Armee.

The bridge over the Maas near Gennep on 10 May 1940 after it was prevented from being blown up ahead of the advance of 18. Armee.

ALS FÜHRER DES I. BATL. (Lehr-Rgt. z. b. V. 800)
Mein Wechsel zum Baulehrbtl. z. b. V. 800 (Div. Brandenburg)
Hochzeit Oblt. Dr. Herzner Dez. 40

AS LEADER OF I. BATAILLON (Lehr-Regiment z.b.V. 800)
My transfer to the Bau-Lehr-Bataillon z.b.V. 800 (Division Brandenburg)
Wedding of Oblerleutnant Dr. Herzner [in] December 1940

In August 1939, Leutnant Hans-Albrecht Herzner led the first Abwehr commando raid in Poland. He was compelled to withdraw after a brief action, having learned that the planned German invasion was not underway after all, but had been postponed until September.

Kas. Brand. Jan. 41.

Brandenburg Barracks, January 1941.

Chapter Three

The Balkans: 1941

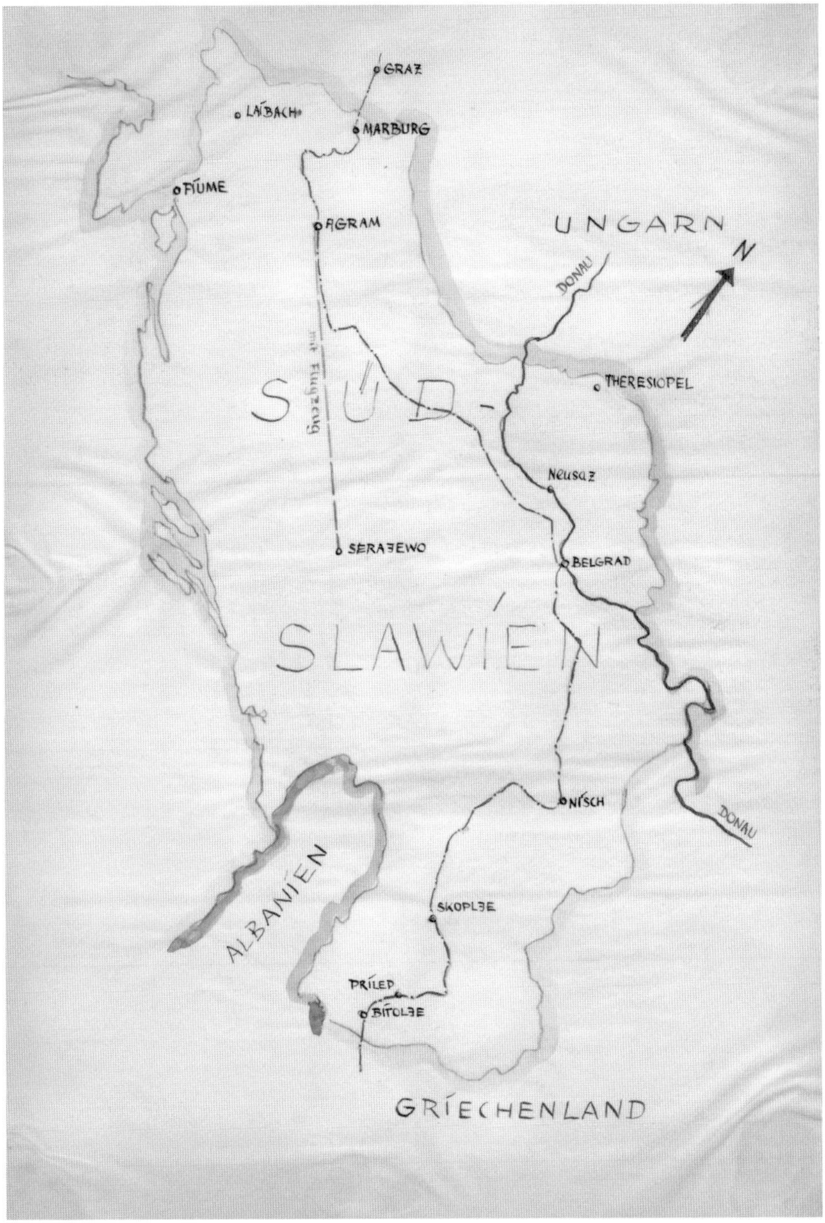

DER BALKANFELDZUG 1941
THE BALKANS CAMPAIGN 1941

(**Above**) Sonderkraftfahrzeug *(half-track) and heavy artillery piece of Artillerie-Regiment 74.*

(**Below**) Haeling [sic: Haehling] v. Lanzenauer
Obstlt u. Kdr. Lehr-Rgt. BR.

Haehling von Lanzenauer
Oberstleutnant and commander of Lehr-Regiment BR ['Brandenburg'].

Oberstleutnant (later Generalmajor) Paul Haehling von Lanzenauer commanded the Brandenburger from 30 November 1940 until his death from natural causes in February 1943.

Me 109 [sic: 108]
Messerschmitt Bf 108

(**Above**) MARBURG

This crossing, known by various names, including Old Bridge, spanned the River Sava at Maribor, in present-day Slovenia.

(**Below**) AGRAM

Present-day Zagreb, in Croatia.

Latin Bridge, Sarajevo, Bosnia.

SERAJEWO

SARAJEVO

Note Serbian Adrian helmets placed atop each bivouac.

King Alexander Bridge, in Belgrade, demolished in a futile effort to stem advancing German forces.

Destroyed bridge, probably in the copper-mining area of Bor, in eastern Serbia.

(**Above**) GRIECHENLAND
GREECE

(**Below**) AM PIRÄUS
AT PIRAEUS

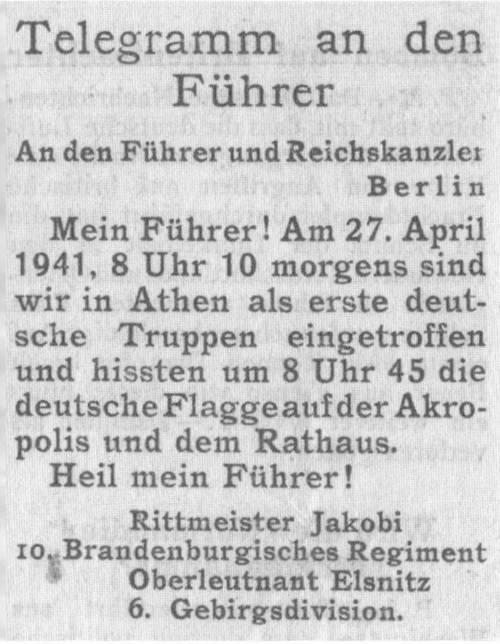

Telegramm an den Führer

An den Führer und Reichskanzler
Berlin

Mein Führer! Am 27. April 1941, 8 Uhr 10 morgens sind wir in Athen als erste deutsche Truppen eingetroffen und hissten um 8 Uhr 45 die deutsche Flagge auf der Akropolis und dem Rathaus.

Heil mein Führer!

Rittmeister Jakobi
10. Brandenburgisches Regiment
Oberleutnant Elsnitz
6. Gebirgsdivision.

(**Left**) Telegram to the Führer

To the Führer and Reich Chancellor
Berlin

My Führer! On 27 April 1941, at 8:10 in the morning, we were the first German troops to arrive in Athens and at 8:45. we raised the German flag on the Acropolis and the Town Hall.

Hail my Führer!

Rittmeister Jakobi
10. Brandenburgisches Regiment
Oberleutnant Elsnitz
6. Gebirgsdivision.

(**Opposite**) Deutsche Landser an der Ägäis [1941]
Die griechischen Schuhputzer hatten rasch bemerkt, dass der deutsche Soldat die Reinlichkeit liebt. Hier haben sie auf der Universitäts = Strasse von Athen, einen Ritterkreuzträger (Walther) „in der Arbeit".

German troops in the Aegean [1941]
The Greek shoe shiners quickly noticed that the German soldier loves cleanliness. Here you have a Knight's Cross bearer (Walther) 'in the works' on University Street of Athens.

(**Below**) *Identification card for entering Athens.*

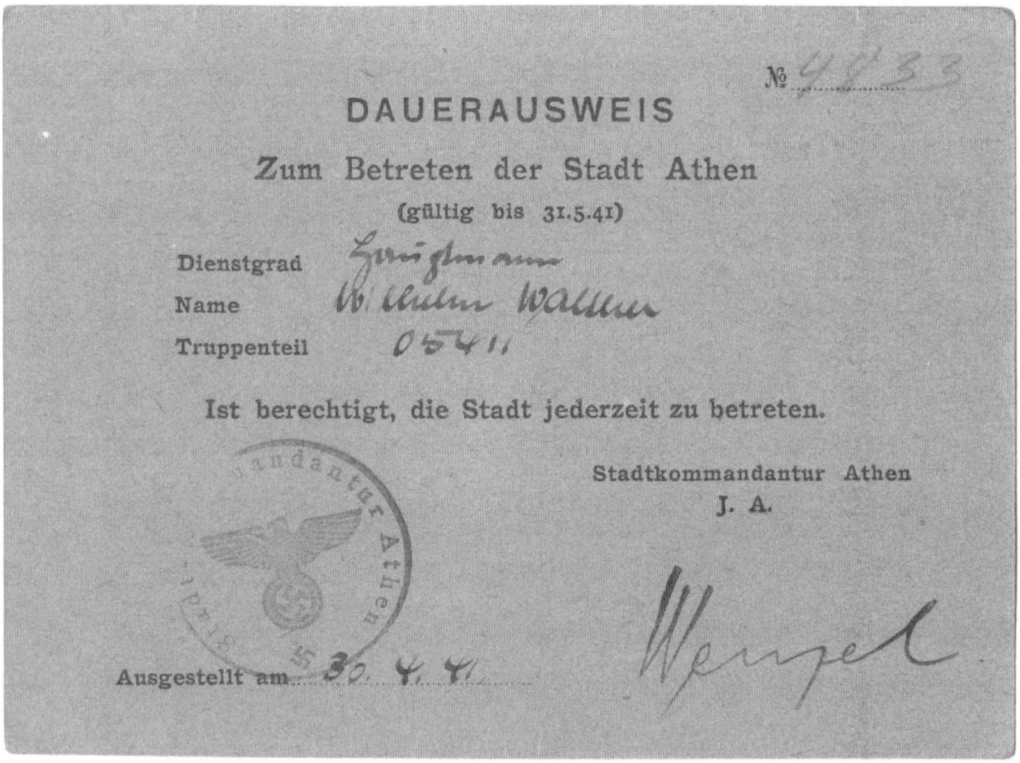

№ 4833

DAUERAUSWEIS

Zum Betreten der Stadt Athen

(gültig bis 31.5.41)

Dienstgrad
Name Wilhelm Walther
Truppenteil 05411

Ist berechtigt, die Stadt jederzeit zu betreten.

Stadtkommandantur Athen
J. A.

Wenzel

Ausgestellt am 30. 4. 41

Wehrmacht victory parade in Athens on 3 May 1941.

Chapter Four

Russia: 1941–42

1941
1. Haeling [sic: Haehling] v. Lanzenauer Kdr. Lehr-Rgt.
2. Lt. Dr. Herzner
3. Maj. [Friedrich-Wilhelm] Heinz

1941
1. Haehling von Lanzenauer commanding Lehr-Regiment
2. Leutnant Dr. Herzner
3. Major [Friedrich Wilhelm] Heinz

It is unclear if this photograph was taken during the 1941 Balkans offensive or at the start of Operation 'Barbarossa' in summer 1941. (Friedrich Wilhelm Heinz would be implicated in the July 1944 plot to assassinate the Führer. He went into hiding and survived the war.)

(**Opposite above**) „Pz. Gr. 4"
Generaloberst Höppner [sic: Erich Hoepner] Befehlshaber 4. Pz. Armee mit. Chef d. Stabes [Generalfeldmarschall Wilhelm Ritter von Leeb]

'Panzergruppe 4'
Generaloberst [Erich] Hoepner commanding 4. Panzerarmee with Chief of Staff [Generalfeldmarschall Wilhelm Ritter von Leeb]

Erich Hoepner was dismissed from the Wehrmacht as a result of Adolf Hitler's displeasure with his performance on the Eastern Front in winter 1941/42. Implicated in the July 1944 Hitler assassination plot, he was sentenced to death and hanged on 8 August 1944. After the war, Wilhelm Ritter von Leeb was tried at Nuremberg and sentenced to three years' imprisonment as a consequence of his knowledge of the Barbarossa Jurisdiction Order. He died in Bavaria on 29 April 1956.

(**Above**) Lagebesprechung

Briefing

Photograph thought to have been taken at Ultena, Lithuania, in June 1941. Left to right: Oberst Walter Chales de Beaulieu (later Generalleutnant, died on 26 August 1974), Generalfeldmarschall von Leeb, Generaloberst Hoepner and Oberst Günther Angern (later Generalleutnant, thought to have committed suicide to avoid being taken prisoner at Stalingrad in February 1943).

beim A. K. General [Erich] v. Manstein

At A.K. [Armee Kommandeur?] General [Erich] von Manstein

(**Below**) Beim Kaffee mahlen
Grinding coffee

An der Luga, vor Leningrad zusammen mit Hptm Grabert († 1942) Sommer 1941

On the Luga [river], in front of Leningrad, together with Hauptmann Grabert († 1942). Summer 1941

Siegfried Grabert was one of only three Brandenburger to win the Knight's Cross with Oak Leaves. He had been awarded the Knight's Cross after securing a bridge and preventing its demolition in Axioupoli, northern Greece, in April 1941. On 25 July 1942, Grabert led an operation near Bataysk, in Russia, to seize a vital causeway across the Don river. The operation was a success, but cost Grabert his life. He was awarded the Oak Leaves posthumously.

Stützpunkt a. d. Rollbahn Nord

Strongpoint on the Rollbahn north

Used especially on the Eastern Front, the Rollbahn *was a main supply route.*

(**Below**) Durch endlose Wälder des Baltikum
Through the endless forests of the Baltic States

(**Above**) Hptm. [Werner] John u. Lt. Andreß

Hauptmann [Werner] John and Leutnant Andreß

(**Left**) *Detail of unit sign on rear of vehicle.*

(**Above**) Panzerbüchse
Anti-tank rifle

(**Below**) Scharfschiessen
Sharp shooting

(**Below**) Adju. [Hans] Gerlach [links]
Adjutant [Hans] Gerlach [left]

Hauptmann Gerhard Pinckert.

Beute-Panzer

Tank booty

Russian T-34 (above) and T-35 tanks.

This and the next three photographs appear to have been taken on 15 March 1942 – Heldengedenktag (Heroes Remembrance Day) – in Brandenburg an der Havel.

(**Below**) *One of several images dated 16 June 1942. Adrian von Foelkersam, far left, facing camera.*

Chapter Five

Russia: 1942–43

Off. meines Stabes
N.O. Kress Kv. Rat [Kriegsverwaltungsrat] Müller Adju. Etteler

Officers of my staff
Nachrichtenoffizier Kress, [Kriegsverwaltungsrat] Müller, Adjutant Etteler

Nachrichtenoffizier *was the signal or intelligence officer.* Kriegsverwaltungsrat *(war administrator) was a title held by a civil servant in the Wehrmacht during the Second World War, and corresponded to the rank of major. Later in the war, Hans Etteler was seriously wounded, resulting in the loss of a lower leg. He survived Russian captivity and after the war returned to live in Paderborn.*

(**Above**) Lt. Hein †, Hptm. [Siegfried] Grabert †, x [Walther], Lt [Karl?] Renner

(**Right**) Grab Grabert Donbrücke b. Bataisk. 1942

Grave [of] Grabert [area of the] Don Bridge near Bataysk. 1942

Ritterkreuzträger
Hauptm. Siegf. Grabert
Feldp. Nr. 03271, † 25.7.42
Ltn. Oskar Müller
Feldp. Nr. 03271, † 25.7.42

Feldw. Haar, Lt. Schatz

Grab Schatz a. Kaukasus 1942

Grave [of] Schatz in the Caucasus 1942

Oberleutnant Oskar Schatz, from Swakopmund, South West Africa (present-day Namibia), was killed in the Terek region on 22 August 1942.

(**Above**) Gen. Oberst Hot [sic: Hoth, rechts] m. Gen. Stab 4. Pz. Armee 1942

Generaloberst Hot [sic: Hoth, right] with General Staff 4. Panzerarmee 1942

Generaloberst Hermann Hoth would be tried for war crimes at Nuremberg and handed a fifteen-year custodial sentence. He was released in 1954, and died on 25 January 1971.

WH
Fp.N.38136
2-10 V
G3234

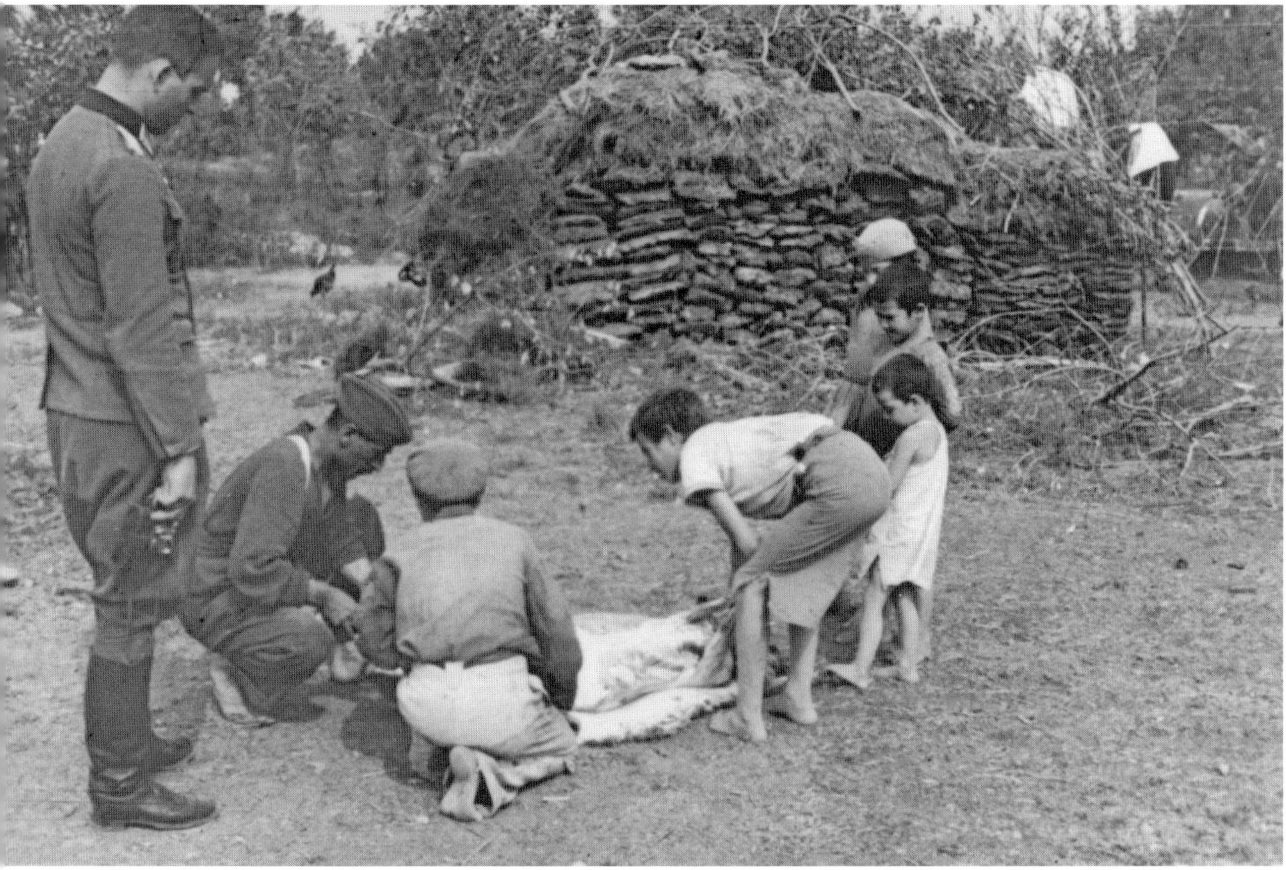

(**Above**) Auf dem Vormarsch zum Kaukasus
Sommer 1942

During the advance to the Caucasus
Summer 1942

(**Below**) Tarn-Kommando vorm Einsatz in russ. Uniformen

Camouflage [i.e. disguised] commando before deployment in Russian uniforms

Mein Adju. vor seinem letzten Einsatz am Baksan
My adjutant before his last assignment at Baksan

(**Above**) mit Lt. v. Foelkersam u. Oblt. Behrend (N.O.)

With Leutnant von Foelkersam and Oberleutnant Behrend (Nachrichtenoffizier)

Adrian Freiherr von Foelkersam was from an aristocratic Baltic German family with a distinguished record of service to the Russian Empire. In 1944, he transferred from the Brandenburger to Otto Skorzeny's SS-Jägdverbände. He was fluent in German, Russian and, according to Skorzeny, French and English. Seriously wounded in January 1945 in the area of Hohensalza (today Inowrocław in Poland), the ultimate fate of this much-respected officer is uncertain. Possibly, he was taken prisoner by the Soviets and died while in captivity.

(**Below**) Terek – Kosaken

Terek – Cossacks

(**Above**) Der Kaukasus
Der umgeleitete „Lenin-Kanal"

The Caucasus
The redirected 'Lenin Canal'

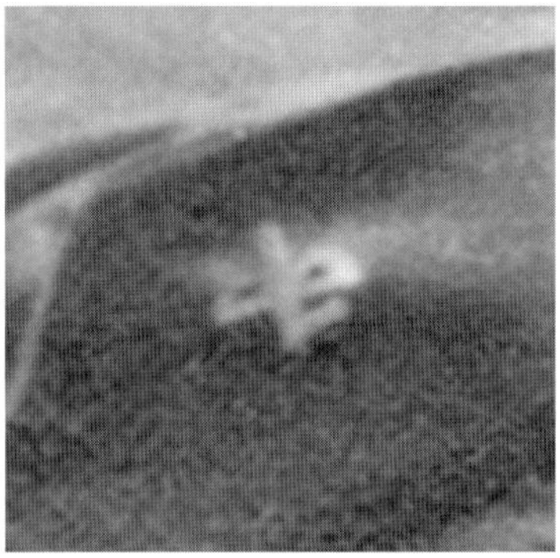

(**Right**) *Detail showing Walther's cap badge, indicating 'Gruppe Walther'. This same motif was later adopted for 1. Regiment 'Panduren' ['Pandurs'].*

(**Below**) mit N.O. Oblt. Behrend

With Nachrichtenoffizier Oberleutnant Behrend

(**Below**) *Sign above a dug-out: 'Mousehole'.*

(**Above**) mit „Stabsgans Marianne"

With 'Staff goose Marianne'

Note 'housekeeping' arrangement: racked hand grenades and the notice: 'Order prevails here'.

(**Below**) Kp. Chef Hptm. John u. Russin Maria

Company commander Hauptmann John and Russian Maria

Shown outside the same bunker as in the previous image, Maria was a Russian prisoner of war who volunteered to work for her captors in an intelligence-gathering role. She is thought to have later married a Brandenburger and resettled in Germany.

Gruppe
Walther

Ritterkreuzverleihung an Lt. von Foelkersam Sept. 1942

Award of Knight's Cross to Leutnant von Foelkersam, September 1942

Generalmajor Franz Westhoven of 3. Panzer-Division presents Leutnant von Foelkersam with the Knight's Cross for his role in preventing the Soviets from damaging oilfield installations as German forces pushed towards the Maykop area, east of the Black Sea. Among those attending the award ceremony are a number of 'Brandenburg' Fallschirmjäger.

(**Above**) *The notice is a warning to drive slowly so as to avoid creating dust and attracting artillery fire. The caption on the back of this photo appears to read:* Am Terek Okt. 43. *If this is the Terek region, the year is 1942.*

(**Opposite below and the following three images**) Absetzbewegungen über d. Asowsche Meer zur Krim
Winter 1942

Withdrawal over the Sea of Azov to Crimea
Winter 1942

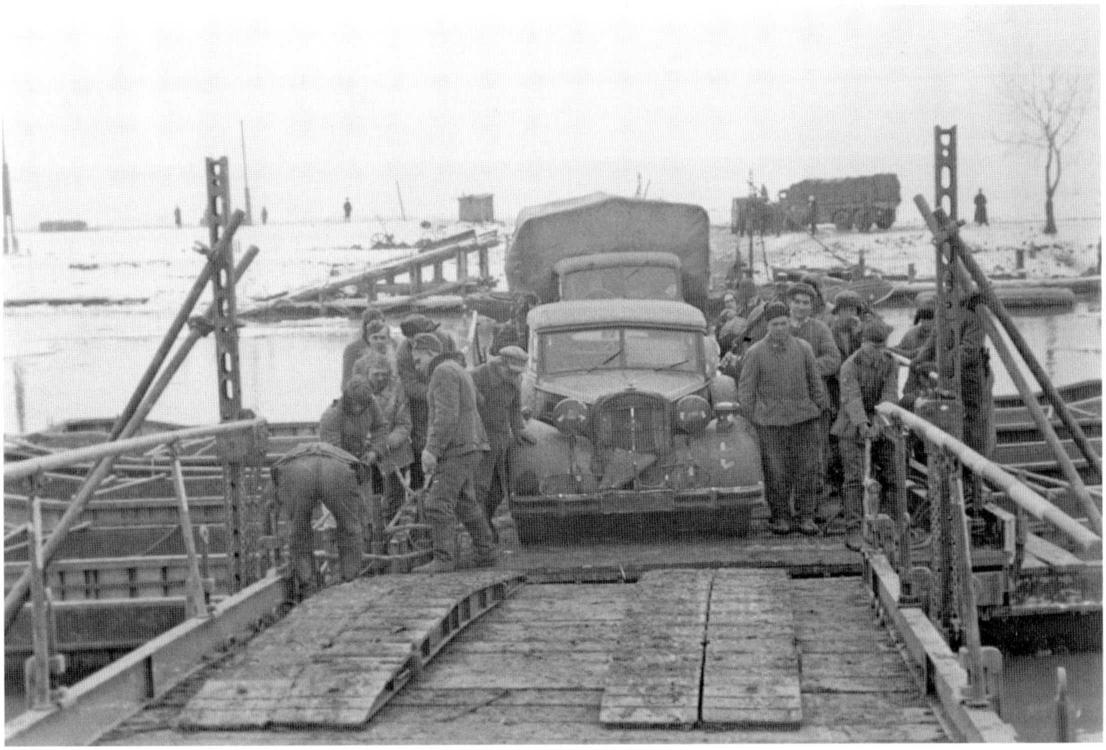

(**Below**) Auf der Krim
In the Crimea

(**Above**) Bahntransport Richtung Heimat

Rail transport towards home

(**Below**) Unsere Toten, die wir zurücklassen mussten Soldatenfriedhof a. d. Krim (heute verwüstet und eingeebnet)

Our dead, we had to leave behind [at the] military cemetery in the Crimea (today devastated and levelled)

2. Juni 1943 11^{47} Abf. n. Russland (Nord)
Das Off. Korp

2 June 1943 11:47 Departure to Russia (North)
The Officer Corps

This and the following four photographs were taken at Freiburg, in Germany, as officers were departing for Siwerskaja, south of Leningrad. Among those who have gathered to bid them farewell is Walther's wife, Eva-Isolde (with headscarf, page 116).

3
Offz.

Siwerskaja a. d. Karelischen Grenze Nordabschnitt Russland

Siwerskaja on the Karelian border, northern sector, Russia

For several weeks in summer 1943, Wilhelm Walther was engaged in anti-partisan operations in the area of Siwerskaja, south of Leningrad. The officer on the far left is Adrian Freiherr von Foelkersam.

Chapter Six

Greece: 1943–44

The images in this section are from some of the last pages in Wilhelm Walther's photo album, where they often appear quite haphazardly, frequently undated and without detailed captions.

Niketempel [Griechenland]
Temple of Athene Nike [Greece]

Btln. Hollmann in Levadia zur Besichtigung angetreten

Beginning inspection of Bataillon Hollmann in Livadeia

Wilhelm Hollmann, thought to have been a Hauptmann *at the time he commanded I./4. Regiment in Greece. He is seen walking alongside Wilhelm Walther.*

(**Above**) Kämpfe im Parnass

Fighting in Parnassus

(**Below**) Am Scherenfernrohr m. Oblt. [Max] Wandrey
Sommer 1943 in Griechenland

On the telescopic sight with Oberleutnant [Max] Wandrey
Summer 1943 in Greece

L.G. 42 (Leichtgesch.) u. PaK in Feuerstellung
Kampf in den Bergen gegen Partisanen [Griechenland, 1943]

L.G. 42 (Leichtgeschütz) and PaK in action
Fighting partisans in the mountains [Greece, 1943]

The Panzerabwehrkanone 40, or PaK 40, was a 7.5cm anti-tank gun; the L.G.42 was a 10.5cm recoilless weapon.

(**Above**) Rgt. Gef. Stand in [unlesbar] (Kithairon-geb.) Anf. Aug. 1943.
Regimental command post in [unreadable] (Kithairon mountains), early August 1943.

(**Below**) Auf einem Min. Räum-Boot i. d. Ägäis mit Admiral [Werner] Lange
Nov. 43
On a minesweeper in the Aegean Sea with Admiral [Werner] Lange
November 1943

(**Above**) Rückeroberung der Insel Leros (Ägäis) Herbst 1943
Recapture of the island of Leros (Aegean) autumn 1943
This is Alinda Bay, as seen from Meraviglia, where British command headquarters was located.

(**Below**) *Castello feature, seen from a gun position on Meraviglia.*

(**Above**) *Below an Italian gun position atop Meraviglia: British and Italian field graves.*

(**Left and opposite**) Gen. Müller, 22. Luftlande-Div. – nach dem Krieg von den Griechen ermordet.

General Müller, 22. Luftlande-Division – murdered by the Greeks after the war.

Generalleutnant Friedrich-Wilhelm Müller would be taken prisoner by the Soviets in East Prussia. Accused of war crimes committed during his command on Crete, he was handed over to the Greeks, found guilty, and executed on 20 May 1947.

(**Above**) Schnellbootflotille
Ägäis
Als Parlamentär nach Samos

Schnellboot flotilla
Aegean
As negotiator to Samos

E-Boats S 54 and S 55 (above), which conveyed Major Walther's delegation to Samos in order to arrange the surrender of Italian forces, bringing to a conclusion autumn 1943 operations in the Aegean.

(**Below**) *Italians caught while attempting to flee Leros.*

Mit Schnellbooten auf Kurs Samos

With Schnellbooten [E-Boats] on course for Samos

Oberleutnant zur See Horst Weber, commander of S 55 *(he would survive the war).*

An initial attempt to reach the island by E-Boat was met with gunfire. Major Walther reached the port of Tigani the next day, 22 November 1943. On arrival, the German delegation were met by a British officer. Walther would recall: 'He was a typical commando type, very dashing, but unfortunately no use to me as apparently he "didn't know anything", he didn't even know about an island commandant.' The identity of the officer has not been established.

(**Above**) S 54 *at Tigani on 22 November 1943.*

(**Below**) Übergabeverhandlungen mit dem ital. Insel-Kommandenten

Surrender negotiations with the Italian island commandant

When the negotiating Italian officer enquired if it was really necessary to surrender those who had womenfolk on the island, Walther was unmoved, responding with, 'Matey, if one surrenders, it generally means everybody.'

(**Above**) *This and the next two photographs were taken in or about December 1943 during a visit by Generalmajor Alexander von Pfuhlstein, who succeeded Oberstleutnant von Lanzenauer and commanded the Brandenburger until April 1944. Imprisoned after being implicated in the 20 July 1944 bomb plot, he would survive the war, surrendering to American forces at Wertheim, Germany, on 2 April 1945.*

(**Opposite**) Der historische Augenblick.
RK f. Wandrey
1943 Lamia – Griechenland
v. links n. re.: Gen. Felmy, Kd. Gen. 67. AK [LXVII. Armeekorps].
Wandrey
Walther

The historic moment.
Knight's Cross for Wandrey
1943 Lamia – Greece
From left to right: General Felmy, commanding general LXVII. Armeekorps.
Wandrey
Walther

Max Wandrey was presented with the Knight's Cross on 9 January 1944. In February 1945, Wandrey, by this time a Major, was fatally wounded; he was posthumously awarded the Oak Leaves to his Knight's Cross. After the war, Hellmuth Felmy would be accused of war crimes and tried at Nuremberg; he was sentenced to fifteen years' imprisonment, but freed in 1951. He died in Darmstadt, Germany, on 14 December 1965.

These images and those on the next two pages appear to show anti-partisan operations in the area of Mount Parnassus, Greece, possibly in December 1943.

WH

WH

Stabsarzt Dr. [Hans] Karsch, [Walther], Wandrey.
Griechenland, Winter 1943

Medical Officer Dr. [Hans] Karsch, [Walther], Wandrey.
Greece, winter 1943

Chapter Seven

Albania and Yugoslavia: 1944

Verlegung des 1. Rgt. nach Norden
Relocation of 1. Regiment to the north

(**Below**) *Skanderbeg Square, Tirana, Albania, c. March 1944.*

The Balkans, mid-1944.

(**Above**) Generallt. Kühlwein beim 1. Rgt. auf Terrasse Kdr. Wohnung Skradin

At 1. Regiment Generalleutnant Kühlwein on the terrace of the commander's apartment Skradin

Skradin, in present-day Croatia. Generalleutnant Friedrich (Fritz) Kühlwein, who succeeded Generalmajor von Pfuhlstein as divisional commander in April 1944, would in turn be succeeded by Oberst (later Generalmajor) Hermann Schulte-Heuthaus later the same year. All three would survive the war.

(**Below**) Stabsgebäude in Skradin – Sommer 1944

Staff building in Skradin – summer 1944

Building photographed in more recent times.

(**Above**) Mit General [sic: Generalleutnant] Kühlwein an den Krka-Wasserfällen
Mai 1944
Dalmatien.

With Generalleutnant Kühlwein at the Krka Waterfalls
May 1944
Dalmatia.

(**Left**) Kdr. mit Adju. [Hans] Etteler

Commander with Adjutant [Hans] Etteler

auf Tito-Jagd in Bosnien

Hunting for Tito in Bosnia

Operation 'Rösselsprung' was conducted in late May 1944, with the primary objective of killing or capturing partisan leader Josip Broz Tito. After fleeing from his base at Drvar, Bosnia, Tito was airlifted to Italy, before establishing a new partisan headquarters on the Adriatic island of Vis.

(**Below**) Ein alter Bosniak muß Auskunft geben
An old Bosniak must provide information

(**Above**) Rgt. Stoßtrupp des 1. Rgt. in Berlin im Sommer 1944 eingeladen von Dr. Goebels [sic] als Anerkennung für Erfolge in Jugoslawien.

Regiment shock troop of 1. Regiment in Berlin in summer 1944, invited by Dr. Goebbels in recognition of successes in Yugoslavia.

This photo appears to have been taken in August 1944, when the unit was presented with the 'Brandenburg' cuff title.

(**Right**) Detail from above image, showing a Brandenburger decorated with the Iron Cross 1st and 2nd Class, Infantry Assault Badge, Wound Badge and Ostvolkmedaille (Eastern People's Medal).

Chapter Eight

Comrades in Arms

Oberstleutnant Wilhelm Walther.

Albert Kunz [sic], Pz. AA.5
gestorben 1956

Albert Kunz [sic], Pz. A.A.5
Died 1956

Albert Kuntz served with Wilhelm Walther in A.A.5, and later took command of Panzer-Aufklärungs-Abteilung 2, being awarded the Knight's Cross in February 1944. He died in 1965.

Rolf von Bünau AA5
gefallen in Russland

Rolf von Bünau A.A.5
Fell in Russia

Another who had served in A.A.5, Hauptmann Rudolf von Bünau was in command of Panzer-Aufklärungs-Abteilung 9 when he was awarded the Knight's Cross on 8 August 1943. He was killed just one week later, near Roslavl, on the Eastern Front, being posthumously promoted to Major.

(**Above**) Siegfried Grabert RK m. Eichenlaub
gef. in Russland 1942

Siegfried Grabert, Knight's Cross with Oak Leaves
Fell in Russia in 1942

(**Opposite**) Mein Ord. Off. 1941 Konrad v. Leipzig
Südwestafrikaner Ritterkreuzträger Kdr. der Küstenjägerabt. Freitod März [sic] 1945

My Ordnance Officer [in] 1941 Konrad von Leipzig
South West African Knight's Cross holder [and] Commander of the Küstenjägerabteilung. Suicide March [sic] 1945

Konrad von Leipzig was one of three brothers. One was in the Luftwaffe; another was Erwin Rommel's personal driver before becoming an officer and joining the Division 'Brandenburg' in 1943. Konrad (sometimes spelled Conrad) had lost a leg while serving in the Wehrmacht earlier in the war. Choosing to remain in uniform, he joined the Brandenburger, leading a long-range reconnaissance unit in North Africa, before going on to command the Küstenjäger. Konrad von Leipzig died in January 1945. It is generally accepted that he took his own life, although the circumstances are unclear. It may have been to escape the relentless pain of his amputation, or to avoid the consequences of being captured by Tito's partisans during operations in the area of Fiume (present-day Rijeka, in Croatia).

Otto Skorzeny, Kdr. der SS Jagdverbände Duce-Befreier, gestorben 1976
Otto Skorzeny, commanding the SS-Jagdverbände, liberator of [Il] Duce, died in 1976

Chapter Nine

Hie guet Brandenburg allewege

Eva-Isolde, a war widow, married Wilhelm on 23 December 1940.

Urlaubsfreuden

Holiday delights

Eva and Wilhelm with their first child, Elke, who was born in 1942.

(**Above**) *Helmet that belonged to Wilhelm Walther – believed to be a memento of his action near Gennep, on 10 May 1940.*

(**Left**) *Wilhelm Walther's wartime awards and decorations included the following:*

10 May 1940: Eiserne Kreuz II (Iron Cross 2nd Class)
10 May 1940: Verwundetenabzeichen in Schwarz (Wound Badge – Black)
26 May 1940: Eiserne Kreuz I (Iron Cross 1st Class)
24 June 1940: Ritterkreuz (Knight's Cross)
1943: Infanteriesturmabzeichen in Silber (Infantry Assault Badge – Silver)
Verwundetenabzeichen in Silber (Wound Badge – Silver)

This charm bracelet, now in the family's possession, would indicate that Walther also received the Dienstauszeichnungen für die Wehrmacht (Wehrmacht Long Service Award) and 1944 Bandenkampfabzeichen (Bandit Warfare, or Anti-Partisan, Badge).

Kriegsgräber-Friedhof in Bourdon b. Amiens mit dem Grab [des] Obslt. G. Erdmann
War graves cemetery in Bourdon near Amiens with the grave of Oberstleutnant G. Erdmann
Wilhelm Walther at the grave of his old comrade and mentor, Oberstleutnant Günther Erdmann, in summer 1991.

Appendix

Wilhelm Walther's Service Record

The following information is derived mainly from the *Personalakten* (personnel records) of Wilhelm Walther and his prisoner information sheet while detained at Dachau in 1947.

Pre-War Service and Promotions

1929–1933
Military courses and Czech border duty (responsible for about 300 men during 1931–33)
Grenzschutz

November 1933
Military Sports Instructor
University of Hamburg

Mid-January–October 1934
Headmaster
SA-Sportschule [SA Sport School] at Trittau, Holstein

1 November 1934
Joined Kraftfahr-Abteilung 5

25 November 1935
Feldwebel der Reserve

1 June 1936
Leutnant der Reserve
Aufklärungs-Abteilung 5 (A.A.5)

1 June 1937
Leutnant (regular service)
A.A.5

1 October 1938
Oberleutnant
A.A.5

Wartime Commands and Promotions 1939–45

26 August 1939–14 March 1940
Zugführer [platoon leader], later Kompanieführer
A.A.5

15 March 1940
Transferred from A.A.5 to Bau-Lehr-Bataillon z.b.V. 800 (took command of 4. Kompanie)

15 March–31 May 1940
Kompanieführer
Bau-Lehr-Bataillon z.b.V. 800

1 June–15 September 1940
Kompaniechef
II./Lehr-Regiment 'Brandenburg' z.b.V 800

16 September–31 December 1940
Bataillonsführer
I./Lehr-Regiment 'Brandenburg' z.b.V 800

1 January–31 October 1941
Offizier z.b.V. und Verbindungsoffizier [Liaison Officer]
Stab/Lehr-Regiment 'Brandenburg' z.b.V 800

1 March 1941
Hauptmann

1 November 1941–31 March 1942
Bataillonsführer
I./Lehr-Regiment 'Brandenburg' z.b.V 800

1 April–19 November 1942
Bataillonskommandeur
I./Lehr-Regiment 'Brandenburg' z.b.V 800

20 November 1942
Appointed Führer of Verband 801 (which was to replace I. Bataillon and would later become Jägerregiment 1 'Brandenburg')

1 February 1943
Major
Regimentsführer
Sonderverbandes 'Brandenburg'

1 May 1944
Oberstleutnant
Regimentskommandeur
Division 'Brandenburg'

March–May 1945
Stabschef [Chief of Staff]
SS-Jagdverbände

Active Service 1939–45

September 1939
A.A.5 (2. Panzer-Division)
Poland: From Slovakia to Tatra, Tarnów (Poland), Rava-Ruska (eastern Ukraine); returning to Eggenburg in Austria.

October–December 1939
Austria: Eggenburg

December 1939–February 1940
Germany: Heidelberg area

February–March 1940
Germany: Kaisersesch area/Eifel

March–May 1940
Germany: Goch near Kleve

10 May 1940
Bau-Lehr-Bataillon z.b.V. 800
Holland
Wounded at Gennep on 10 May 1940

Mid May–June 1940
Germany: Hospital, Kleve

June–September 1940
Austria: Baden near Vienna

October–November 1940
Germany: Hospital, Heidelberg

December 1940–April 1941
1./Lehr-Regiment 'Brandenburg'
Germany: Brandenburg

April 1941
Balkans Campaign

22 June–14 August 1941
2./Lehr-Regiment 'Brandenburg'
Verbinungsoffizier, 4. Panzergruppe
Latvia: Dünaburg and Russia: Pleskau, Lake Ilmen, Luga Sector

August–November/December 1941
Germany: Hospital, Darmstadt

November/December 1941–Late Spring 1942
Germany: Brandenburg

Summer–December 1942
Russia: Kursk, Voronezh, Don and Terek/Caucasus

December 1942–February 1943
Crimea: Mius

February–June 1943
1. Regiment 'Brandenburg'/Jägerregiment 1. 'Brandenburg'
Germany: Freiburg/Breisgau

Mid-1943
Verbindungsoffizier, 1. Armee
Russia: Leningrad area

26 July 1943–February 1944
4. Regiment and Jägerregiment 1. 'Brandenburg'
Greece: Area of Thebes, Lamia, Leros, Samos, Aliartos

February–September 1944
Jägerregiment 1. 'Brandenburg'

Albania: Tirana, Skutari and Yugoslavia: Šibenik, Zara (Zadar); area of Grahowo (possibly Bosansko Grahovo); Skradin

September–October 1944

Jägerregiment 1. 'Brandenburg'

Wounded 1 October, area of Betschkerek (believed to be Groß Betschkerek, Yugoslavia)

October 1944–February 1945

Austria and Germany: Hospitals in Graz, Salzburg and Jugenheim near Darmstadt

March–May 1945

SS-Jagdverbände

Stabschef

Germany: Friedental near Oranienburg; Hof; near Salzburg; Dachstein area (Austrian Alps)